To: Rosemary

From: Cindy

Why Men Make
BAD PETS

· ·

They really ARE from Mars!

Mara Conlon

PETER PAUPER PRESS, INC.
White Plains, New York

Ladies,

You know how it goes. You meet a guy who seems funny, nice, and attractive. You get sucked in by his charm, his wit, his cuteness and cuddly-ness. But THEN, before you know it, you end up with an *impossible-to-train* PET on your hands! And no care-and-feeding instructions are included. It turns out this is *not* a tame critter, but one who leaves a trail of messes during his quest to satisfy an endless appetite for food and other carnal pleasures. With so much required maintenance, it can be a full-time job to have a man in your life!

The bottom line—men are just beastly.

They may live in their own little world—let's just call it Mars—but let's face it, "you can't live with 'em, you can't live without 'em." So what's a girl to do? (Other than cry, that is?) LAUGH!

Here's a comical collection of those universal traits that show *Why Men Make Bad Pets*. Love 'em or leave 'em—or just get a goldfish. But ya gotta admit, just like the animals in these photos, they're still pretty cute—even with all their faults.

Darn it! Their puppy eyes have worked their magic again!

They think they are **God's gift** to the world.

They string
chicks along.

They think puppy eyes will get them out of the doghouse *every* time.

They are *not* the sharpest tools in the shed.

Some of them are still mamas' boys.

They think
motorcycles make
them look cool.

They really **ARE** from Mars!

They have trouble distinguishing between **private** vs. **public** activities.

. . . but they're not.

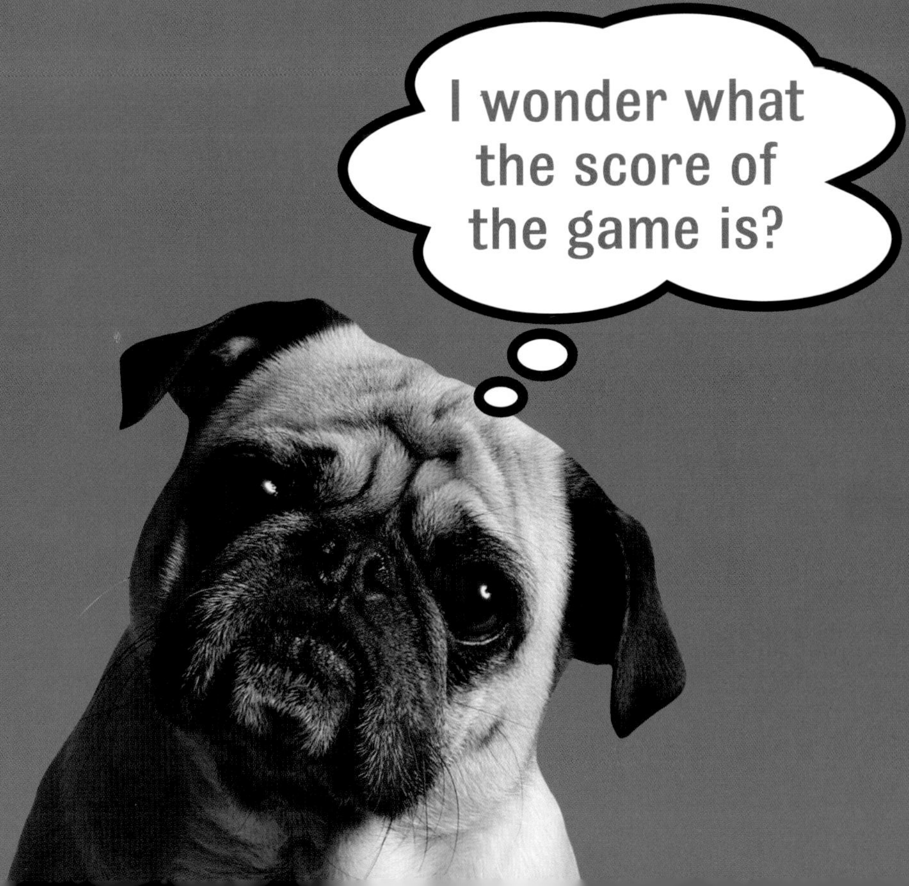

They're not exactly *"subtle"* when checkin' out hot babes.

They have delusions
of grandeur.

One *lit-tle* sign of a cold and they act like they're as sick as a dog.

They'll kiss just about *anything*.

They invented the comb-over.

Their feathers get **ALL** ruffled when you ask them one *little* question!

They are always
trying to cop a feel.

All the good ones
are taken or gay.

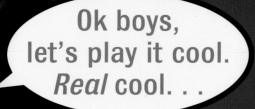

They like to act tough around their friends.

Their brains are two sizes too small.

They're suckers for a
blonde.

They act like *WE'RE* the ones with mood swings??

They don't know how to

ease up on the hair gel.

They act like they have **NO IDEA** how to use a mop.

They can't dress themselves.

They don't like to share.

They get turned on by the *darndest* things!

They want to have their cake, and eat it too.

They give you presents that are **not** on your wish list.

They always
want to fool
around
when you're
trying to
sleep.

They're . . .
too sexy
for their pants.

Some are flashers.

Their idea of a "house in the country" is *very different* from yours.

They think they are "**ALL** that and a bag of chips."

They REFUSE to ask for directions.

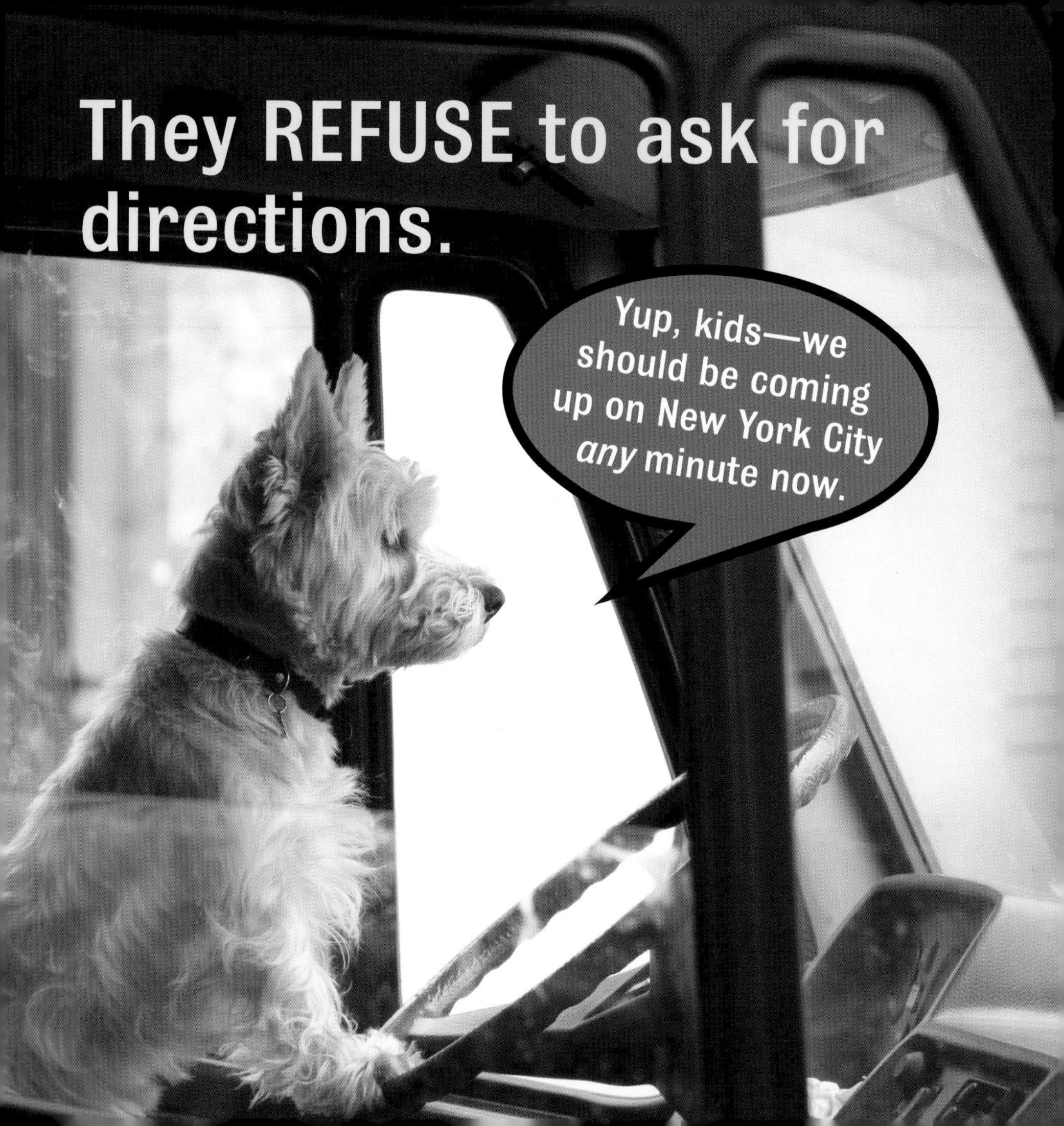

They never want
to share
the remote.

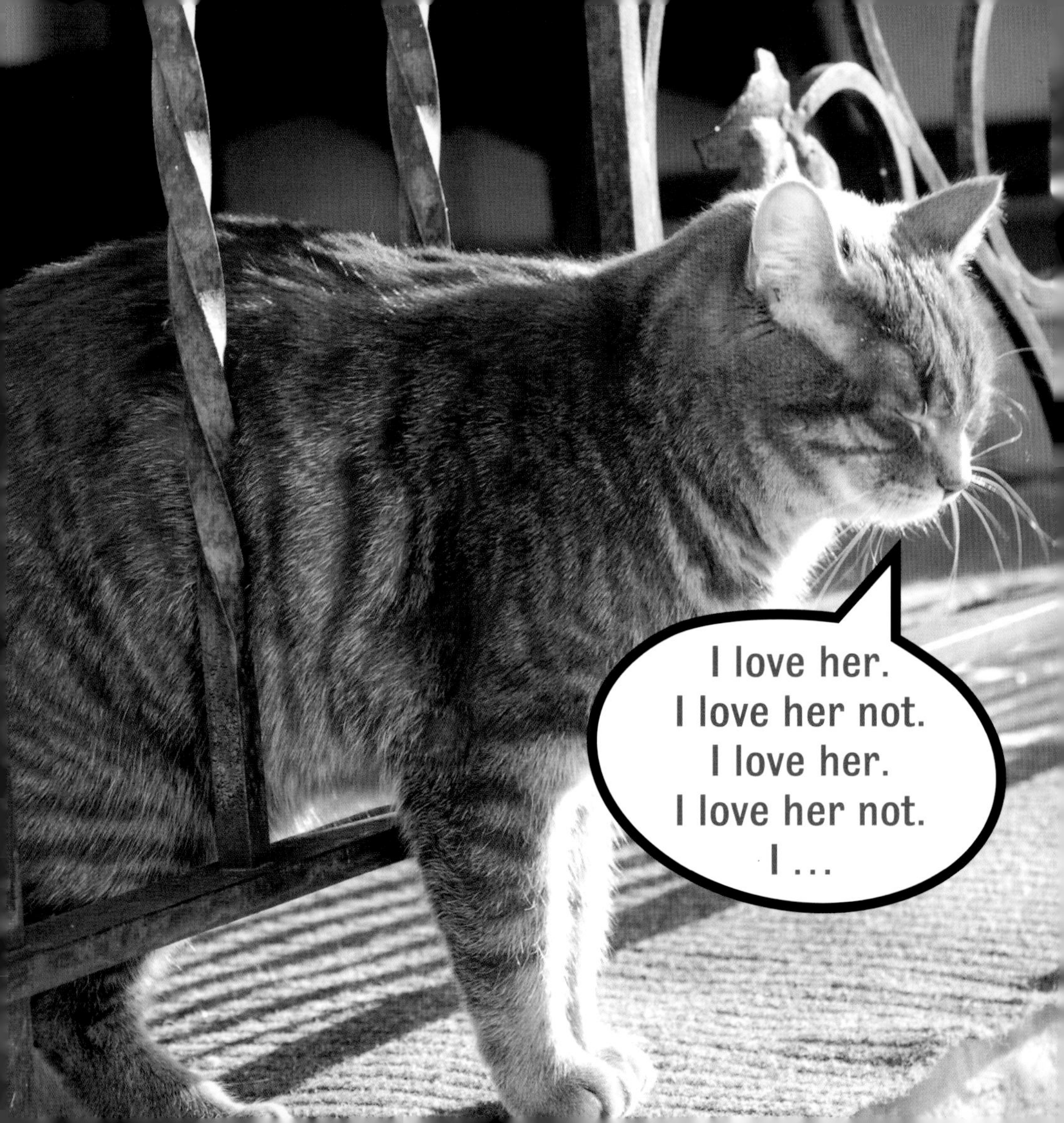
I love her.
I love her not.
I love her.
I love her not.
I ...

They have trouble committing.

They're only interested in the chase.

They're obsessed
with their package.

They *refuse* to talk

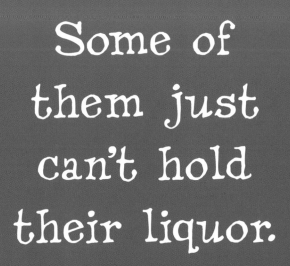

Some of them just can't hold their liquor.

They like to play with their balls.

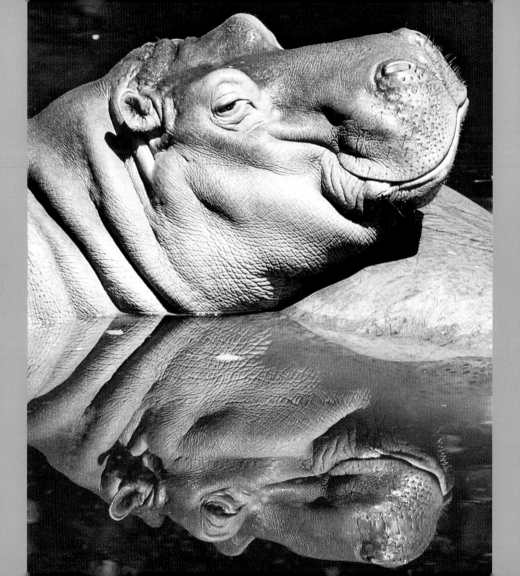

They're so vain, they probably think this book is about **THEM**!

PHOTO CREDITS

Dedicated to all my wonderfully fantastic girlfriends!
You chicks rule!
—mc

A special thanks goes to:

The ever fun-and-clever Megan Leitzinger for her invaluable help on this project!
Leon Dijk of FunnyPetPictures.com for helping me track down some of these photos.
All of the photographers and pet-owners who shared their wonderful photos.
And my fellow Pauperettes who contributed their wit and wisdom, in particular
Barbara Paulding, Suzanne Schwalb, and Evelyn Beilenson.

Designed by La Shae V. Ortiz

Copyright © 2010
Peter Pauper Press, Inc.
202 Mamaroneck Avenue
White Plains, NY 10601
All rights reserved
ISBN 978-1-59359-286-8
Printed in China
7 6 5 4 3 2 1

Visit us at www.peterpauper.com